HOW TO BECOME A PASSIVE INCOME MILLIONAIRE

MAKE MONEY ONLINE

"Absolutely riveting. The easiest, most straight forward guide to earning real money with minimal effort & investment. A real goldmine." – A.T.

ARHAM TANVEER

HOW TO BECOME A PASSIVE INCOME MILLIONAIRE

Copyright © 2020 Arham Tanveer

All rights reserved.

Text Copyright © [Arham Tanveer]
All rights reserved. No part of this guide may be reproduced in any form without permission in writing from the publisher except in the case of brief quotations embodied in articles or reviews.

Legal & Disclaimer
The information contained in this book and its contents is not designed to replace or take the place of any form of medical or professional advice; and is not meant to replace the need for independent medical, financial, legal, or other professional advice or services, as may be required. The information in this book has been provided for educational purposes only.

The content and information contained in this book have been compiled from sources deemed reliable, and it is accurate to the best of the Author's knowledge, information, and belief. However, the author cannot guarantee its accuracy and validity and cannot be held liable for any errors and/or omissions. Further, changes are periodically made to this book as and when needed. Where appropriate and/or necessary, you must consult a professional (including but not limited to your doctor, attorney, financial advisor, or such other professional advisor) before using any of the suggested remedies, techniques, or information in this book.

Upon using the contents and information contained in this book, you agree to hold harmless the Author from and against any damages, costs, and expenses, including any legal fees potentially resulting from the application of any of the information provided by this book. This disclaimer applies to any loss, damages or injury caused by the use and application, whether directly or indirectly, of any advice or information presented, whether for breach of contract, tort, negligence, personal injury, criminal intent, or under any other cause of action.

You agree to accept all risks of using the information presented inside this book. You agree that by continuing to read this book, where appropriate and/or necessary, you shall consult a professional (including but not limited to your doctor, attorney, or financial advisor or such other advisor as needed) before using any of the suggested remedies, techniques, or information in this book.

CONTENTS

Part One: Getting started – Unveiling the Secret Behind Generating Millions in Passive Income! 1

Part Two – How to Use Our Ultra-Secret Method to Make Millions Without Doing Any Work Yourself? 16

Part Three – The Secret behind the Perfect Marketing Pitch: How To Sell More in Less Time? 22

Part FOUR – Launching Your Product: Setting The Course for Success. 37

Part Five – Increase Your Passive Income: Identify patterns to Create Sales Funnels 40

BONU$ SECTION – SHORT, EASY YET EFFECTIVE WAY TO EARN MONEY ONLINE 47

This page is intentionally left blank.

PART ONE: Getting started – Unveiling the Secret Behind Generating Millions in Passive Income!

Overview

In the first section of the book, you will discover the secret way to make a lot of money online – and by the end of this book, you will know everything you need to know how to put this secret way to good use. Who doesn't want to earn honest money with minimal effort in a short time? But when it comes to finding a steady and considerable income stream online, most people do not know how to or where to start.

In this introductory chapter, we will discuss a wide range of subjects – from what Passive income is and how can you use this secret to earn and grow your Passive income from selling eBooks through Amazon's KDP.

ABOUT PASSIVE INCOME MILLIONAIRE

Driven with the vision to empower you with the ultra-secret way of generating passive income online, Passive Income can potentially transform your financial reality. Based on actual experiences, this book will inform you through hard facts and authentic information.

The internet can be a labyrinth – with a humungous influx of information available; it gets quite difficult for people to discern disinformation from actual, valuable knowledge. However, this book will guide you in the right direction – allowing you to build yourself a new life of financial independence!

So, without further ado, let's dive into the secrets of creating (and growing!) your sources of Passive income through the internet.

THE SECRET TO EARNING HUNDREDS OF DOLLARS ONLINE THROUGH PASSIVE INCOME UNVEILED!

Since the advent of eBooks, the sales for paperback and hardcover copies have taken a hit. You won't believe the number of people who are willing to buy eBooks online and read them on their Kindle or other smart devices. **Herein lies a great opportunity** – an opportunity many people have already capitalized upon to earn millions of dollars! The best part? It's all passive, Passive income – which means you won't have to work around to clock to make that money.

Starting from KDP (Kindle Direct Publishing), this book will guide you in a chronological manner – teaching you how to exploit this secret market to millions of dollars.

About Kindle Direct Publishing – What is all the fuss about?

Kindle Direct Publishing (KDP) is a platform created by Amazon, which offers free self-publishing services. Initially known as Digital Text Platform (DTP), Amazon rebranded the self-publishing platform as it grew exponentially within the first year of its conception. In case, you are wondering what self-publishing is, here's a short explanation:

The term **self-publishing** itself is quite self-explanatory. Any book that you publish yourself is considered as 'self-published.' In contrast, conventional notions of book publishing, where you have to either:

a. Earn the approval of a publisher like B&N to publish and print your book,
b. Or you could bear the hefty cost of publishing and printing your own book.

With KDP, you get a great opportunity to publish your book for free and market it to millions of potential customers through Amazon's vast e-commerce network. Gone are the days of spending hefty amounts to publish your book(s). Amazon's Kindle Publishing and several other similar platforms (which will be discussed at length in the next chapters) offer a unique opportunity.

All you need to do is capitalize on it before it's too late. As the age-old proverb says, *'make hay while the sun shines'* – write and sell books as long as the market is not saturated. For now, this secret is known to a few.

STILL NOT CONVINCED? LET'S TALK NUMBERS.

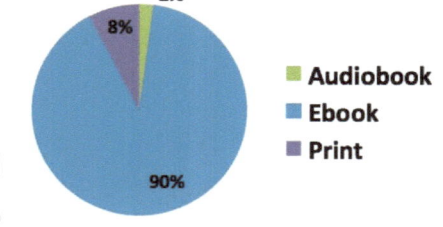

If you are someone who isn't convinced easily, here are some stats for you to realize what a **goldmine** eBook writing is. According to AuthorEarnings.com, eBooks comprised 90% of all book sales in 2019! Paperback books have gone out of vogue for a variety of reasons:

- Environmental factors,
- Increase in printing costs leading to a spike in book prices,
- The advent of smartphones and tablets.

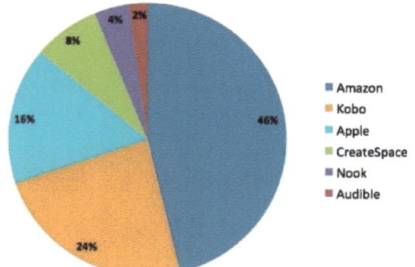

Why KDP?

First of all, it's free. And just because it doesn't charge authors anything for publishing their books, doesn't mean it is the best self-publishing service! Amazon leads the industry with a whopping 46% of the market share. Kobo, Apple, and Nook capture a significant segment of the market too, but why opt for the second-best when you can go for the best in business?

But it is never a smart idea to put all your eggs in one basket. In the next chapter, we discuss how you can use multiple platforms and sources to sell & market your eBook(s).

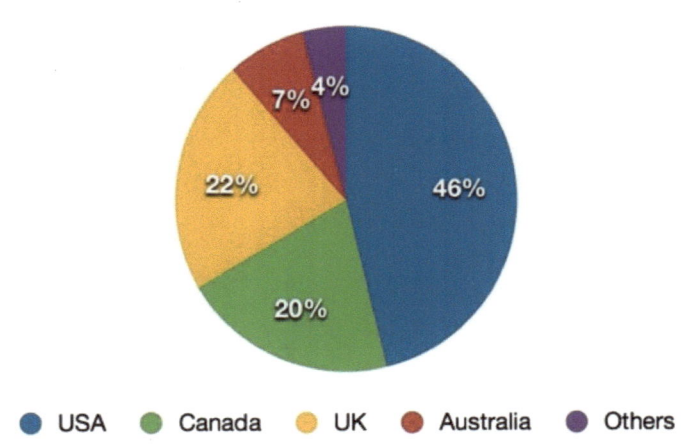

Market Share

No surprises here – North America is the largest market for eBooks. So, it would be ideal for you to write on topics that are relatable to the American and Canadian audiences.

As mentioned earlier, writing with a consumer-centric approach can help you immensely in attracting a larger number of clients. And that's exactly what your objective. The secret to becoming a **Passive Income Millionaire** isn't about working hard – it's about working smart.

Setting Up Your KDP Account

Step #1:

Sign in with your existing Amazon account or create a new KDP account. The signup form is quite concise, requires few details, so it shouldn't take more than a minute or two of your time.

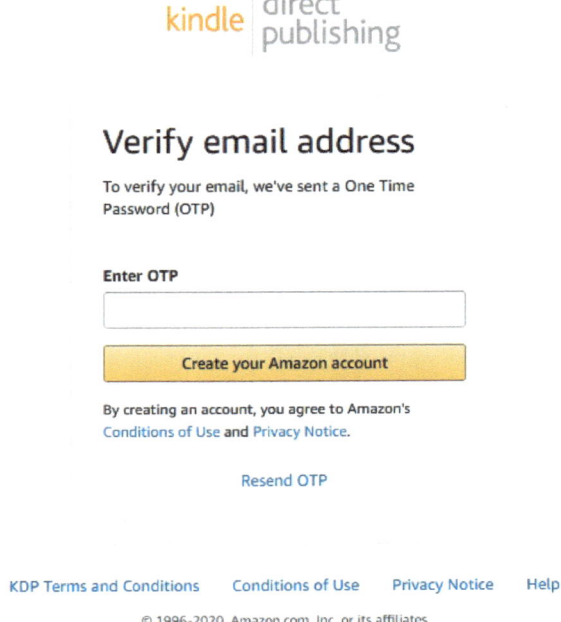

Step #2:

After filling out the signup form, you will be required to verify your email address. Verify your email address by entering the OTP (One Time Password). This OPT will be sent to the email address you entered in the initial form.

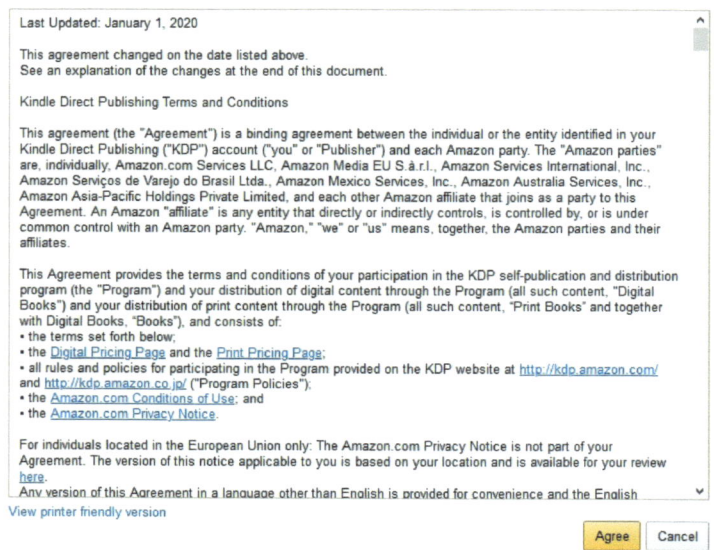

Step #3:

Agree to KDP's terms & conditions after reading them carefully.

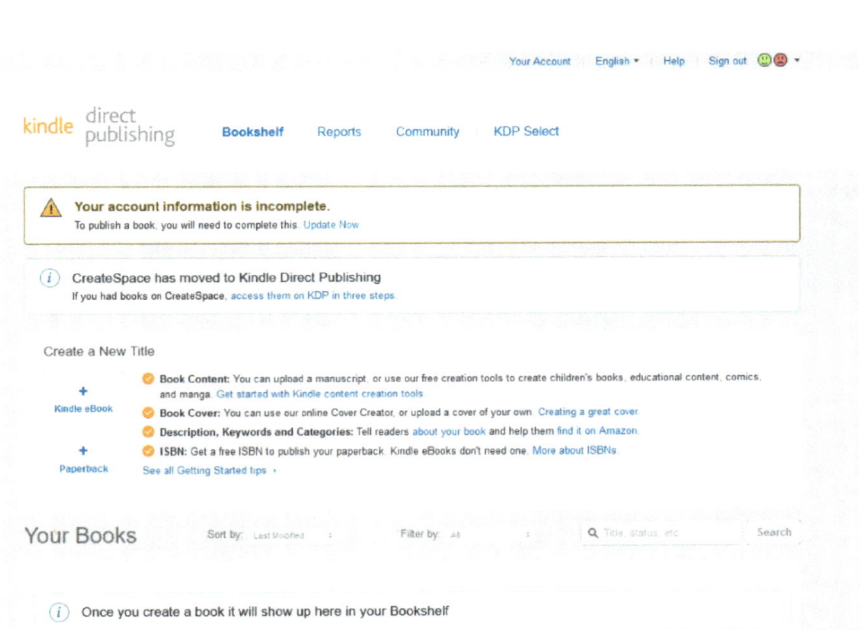

Step #4:

Complete your account information, click on update now.

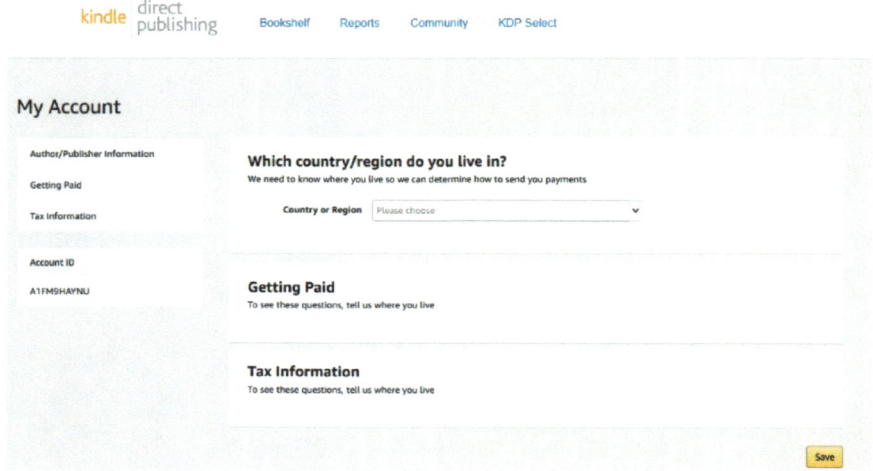

Step #5:

After you click on the 'update now,' you will be redirected to this page. Fill out all fields to complete your account details. Without completing these details, you won't be able to publish and sell books on KDP.

HOW TO BECOME A PASSIVE INCOME MILLIONAIRE

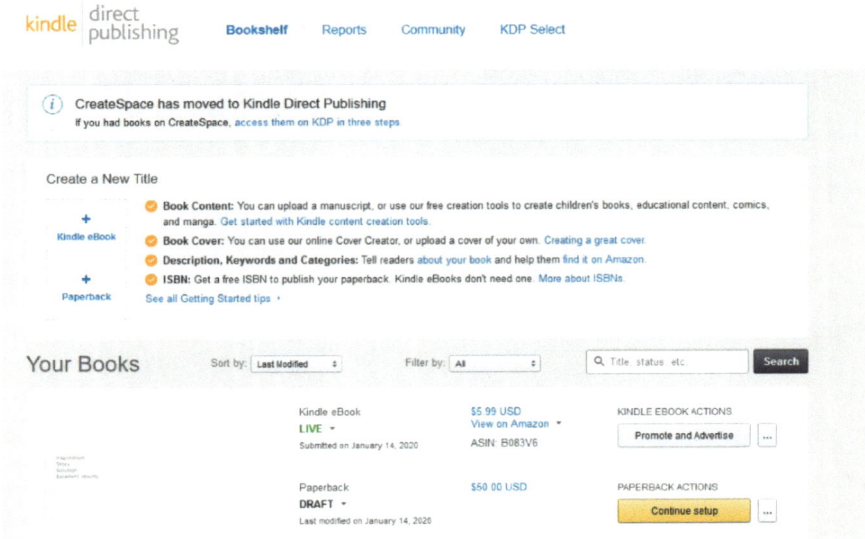

Step #6:

Once you complete and verify all your personal and payment details, you are all set to publish and market your first book with KDP!

Weigh all your options – Make an Informed Choice

KDP is not the only self-publishing platform you can use to publish and sell eBooks. Kobo Writing Life, Nook Press (Barnes & Noble's digital publishing platform), Draft 2 Digital and Smashwords – these are just some of the leading options for authors looking to self-publish their book. But when it comes to publishing costs and exposure, KDP is clearly the best option.

In the previous section, we have already described the signup process for KDP, but in case you wish to use two different platforms – here's how you can create an account on Draft2Digital:

Create a Draft2Digital Account

Sometimes, having an Amazon account is not enough to get started with self-publishing. You may need another account. This account will help in making your book available on various other platforms and sell for free on amazon.

Draft2Digital is an online publishing aggregator that provides distribution and conversion services. It is a great platform to sell your books and make a lot of money online. Once you create an account on Draft2Digital, you are not just confined to Amazon. Through this platform, your book will be listed on many other distribution channels like Kobo, Scribd, Barnes & Nobles, Apple iTunes, with just a click of a button.

Here's a step-by-step guide to creating a draft2digital account:

- **Signup:** Click on signup. A set of specific compulsory fields will appear, where you will have to enter your details. Fill the bars with the correct information and register.
- **Terms & Conditions:** Once you register, a dialogue box will appear. This dialogue box contains all the terms and conditions you might want to know. Click on accept and proceed.
- **Sign-in:** Once you have created your account, you will be asked to sign-in again. Login to your account by entering user credentials.

PART TWO – How to Use Our Ultra-Secret Method to Make Millions Without Doing Any Work Yourself?

Overview

In the second section of the book, you will get to know the secret behind earning money without doing all the hard work yourself. The chapter covers a diverse range of topics that will guide you through the entire process through which you can make others work for you while enjoying a rapid increase in your passive income – becoming a **Passive income millionaire.**

Market Research – Key to Success

Nothing sells like a consumer-centric content. To sell your book and earn millions through self-publishing, it is imperative that you embrace this strategy and execute it smartly. A little research on your niche market before starting your book will significantly improve the outcome. Whatever genre you choose, you should create a book that is unique yet trendy. To understand how to get into action and explore the market, here are some simple steps to make market research a piece of cake.

But what about those who aren't particularly good or interested in writing? If you are one of those, you must be wondering, **"But, hey. I'm not a writer – how will this idea work out for me**?" That's where outsourcing comes in.

Understanding outsourcing

Outsourcing, by definition, is the process of farming out a task to a third-party. From manufacturing businesses to IT firms, most businesses outsource certain aspects of their operations to cut costs, save time, and above all, save themselves the effort of doing everything themselves.

So, you aren't a writer. Or you are a writer but don't have the time to churn out thousands of words every week. **No problem**. Outsource all the hard work to freelancers. Get your work done at a nominal price to save your valuable time and energy. That's outsourcing in a nutshell.

Outsourcing is exactly what you need to make serious money without doing all the work yourself.

How to Outsource Your Work?

Now that you know what outsourcing entails, naturally, your next questions must be where and how I can find people to outsource my work. Twenty years ago, finding the right person to outsource your writing/editing tasks would have been almost impossible. But thanks to the internet and the advent of major freelancing platforms, finding the right people to outsource your work is easier than it was ever before.

- **Where to outsource:**

Fiverr, Guru, and Freelancer.com – all of these platforms are free to sign up for and offer access to millions of talented writers from across the world. You can get your book written, designed, and edited within days for a paltry amount of money. There are so many talented writers on these outsourcing platforms that you would be spoilt for choice.

Fiverr® - The world's largest freelancing platform has the most diverse and vast pool for writers for you to choose from. Writers from all over the world.

Guru – Guru, which derives its name from the Sanskrit word for 'expert,' is one of the top freelancing platforms. Whether you are hunting for a book writer to ghostwrite your book or you want a professional to proofread your book, Guru has just the right person for you.

Freelancer.com – The name of this particular website is quite obvious. It is the mecca for all types of freelancers. From web developers to writers, editors, and designers. Just like Guru or Fiverr, you can find the right person to do all the work for you at a nominal price.

Upwork – With over 12 million freelancers on board, it is impossible for this web site's name to not come up in a conversation about freelancing websites. Although it has far more developers than writers, Upwork is a great place to find writers, designers, and editors for your book.

Since freelancing platforms do not have standardized pricing, it all comes down to your negotiation skills. A 100-page book can cost you anywhere between $100 to $400 dollars. The best thing about hiring in outsourcing the writing process of your book is that you can negotiate the price and verify the quality of work before you pay the writer.

Outsourcing costs

Since freelancing platforms do not have standardized pricing, it all comes down to your negotiation skills. A 100-page book can cost you anywhere between $100 to $400 dollars. The best thing about hiring in outsourcing the writing process of your book is that you can negotiate the price and verify the quality of work before you pay the writer.

"You can publish and sell books for free. You don't even need to write them yourself – you can simply outsource them. In short, you don't need to work hard to potentially earn millions of dollars. So, what's the catch?"

That's the deal – **there's no catch**. Work smart. Earn more. It's as simple as that. But, just to make sure you get it absolutely right, here are the dos and don'ts of outsourcing. Go through them. Consider outsourcing as one of the most integral aspects of the whole Passive income generation process. If you get it right, you are more than halfway there.

PART THREE – The Secret behind the Perfect Marketing Pitch: How To Sell More in Less Time?

Overview

In this section, we will discuss a wide range of subjects – from developing the right marketing strategy to set ambitious yet realistic sales targets; this chapter will cover everything you need to know. While every marketing plan has a similar blueprint, you will realize that every book requires a different marketing approach depending on its genre, niche, and target audience.

The secret to generating Passive income is not just finding an unexplored territory but also planning and executing a smart yet effective marketing strategy. That's exactly what this chapter will unveil. As promised, this book will transform your life by providing you with all the trade secrets of this niche industry. So, without further ado, let's get to it.

Find Trending Genres & Niches

Once you've opted for your category, you can dig into different genres. It would help if you made sure that the niche you're writing for is in-demand and profitable. This knowledge ensures that your genre is trending. Here's the guide to finding a hot niche on amazon:

- Go to www.amazon.com, and on the upper left section, beside the logo, click on 'departments.'
- Click on Kindle E-readers & Books. In the sub-category 'Kindle Store,' click on 'Kindle Books.'
- On the strip below the header, click on bestsellers & more. (A new page will appear)
- Scroll down to 'Category Best Sellers' and click on 'Kindle Best Sellers.'
- On the left section, under Kindle Store, click on 'Kindle eBooks.'
- The section will further expand and display a list of genres.

PRO TIP: ALWAYS MAP OUT YOUR MARKETING STRATEGY BEFORE EVEN STARTING A BOOK. WRITING A BOOK WITH A PRE-CONCEIVED MARKETING APPROACH WILL INCREASE YOUR CHANCES OF SUCCESS EXPONENTIALLY.

Marketing a fictional story

Bookworms around the world are perpetually hungry to read a story that is gripping, enchanting, and at the same time, is narrated in a style that is both eloquent *and* coherent. If done right, a fictional story can make you a millionaire overnight!

The first and only billionaire author, J.K Rowling built her empire by crafting a fictional universe. Take a page out of her book – if you feel your story is compelling and interesting enough, break it down in 3 to 7 books. Stephen King, Suzanne Collins, and Veronica Roth – most famous, successful, and rich authors have used the aforementioned strategy to rope readers in and make millions of dollars.

Marketing a non-fiction book

Non-fiction books have an entirely different target audience altogether. From students to academics and business leaders, the audience for non-fiction is extremely diverse. You can either target a certain niche, let's say, history buffs, by writing a history book, or you could attract a wider audience by going for self-help books.

The Next Step: Choosing a Sub-Category

By now, you ought to have found the genre for your book. To increase its accessibility, you can select a sub-category. A sub-category will help you narrow down the niche of readers and give you further clarity of your target audience. You can check the trending sub-categories through the following steps:

- The Kindle eBooks category expands into a list of genres/main categories.
- Select your main category from the list of Kindle eBooks genres. (e.g., Self-Help)
- You'll see a list of sub-categories right below your primary category. (e.g., creativity, happiness, inner child, and so forth). Choose the sub-category relevant to your story.

The main category is too broad, which makes the book-hunting process vague for the readers. It also expands your target audience unnecessarily. Hence, you need to choose a sub-category carefully, to target a specific group of readers for consistent and long-term royalty.

Fiction & Non-Fiction Ranking

Thousands of books are published every month on Kindle. When you select a category, it is vital that you know how the ranking works on Kindle to shortlist a genre. Here's what's needed to choose a genre.

- **Fiction Ranking:** To determine the competition in Fiction, you must always look for #1 and #100 bestsellers. It gives you a broad range to explore and work. #1 Bestseller can be ranked 2500 and below. It determines how popular the category is and how much money it is making. As the rank descends, the revenue ascends. As for rank #100, look for 25,000 or more. A higher rank corresponds to lower competition.

- **Non-Fiction Ranking:** The elements to look for in non-fiction ranking is different from fiction ranking. When looking for ranking in a non-fiction category, you need to check the sales rank, which should be around 25,000 or less with about 20-25 reviews. (Your primary focus must be on the sales rank. Reviews are just a bonus for value addition). When the book appears to be on a scale of 25,000 or less, the book is trending and has the potential to make serious money for the author.

BIOGRAPHY

Biography & Autobiography

Some people realize the significance of their life experiences and decide to pen them down in an autobiography. But most people don't realize the value of their experiences – maybe you are one of them?! Write your story in a way that inspires others. An autobiography written in an inspirational way can also fall under the category of a self-help book – allowing you to target two market segments.

COMEDY

Comedy

In a world riddled with climatic and political crises, most readers look for respite in comedy. Albeit comedy writing is a daunting task – the dividends it pays makes it quite an attractive proposition. Deploying humor effectively can help you sell thousands of copies!

ROMANCE

Romance

From Shakespeare's Romeo and Juliet to Nicholas Sparks' Notebook, romance is arguably the most popular genre. Chick lit, Young Adult (YA), erotica – this genre encompasses a wide range of sub-categories, each of which has a sizeable audience.

Thriller

Dan Brown, Stephen King, and John Grisham — what do they have in common? All of them have sold millions of copies of their books, both in print and digital versions. Another common denominator among these three authors? They are considered to be the most popular thriller writers.

Whether it's a movie, TV show, or a book — who doesn't like cliffhangers? Thrillers employ suspense, mystery, and drama to intrigue the readers. If you want to establish a large and loyal reader base, this is the perfect genre for you.

Look Up the Best-Selling Authors in Your Selected Category

When writing for Kindle or any other platform, you should look for the top five or ten bestselling authors in your selected genre. Once you list them down, start reading their books. There must be something unique about their work, which makes them bestselling authors.

Other than the story, the elements which make them stand out are the title, book cover, description, market trends, and reviews. Here's why these bestselling authors stand out among the thousands of books published every month:

Title: Bestselling book titles are consistent, engaging, and they relate to the genre. One look at these titles is enough to capture the reader's attention. Treat the title of the book as Call to Action (CTA) – as most readers online have a short attention span. If your title isn't catchy enough to grab their interest, most of them would just simply scroll past it.

Cover: When you analyze the cover of a bestseller, you see that it is creative, sticks to the genre, and the title of the book. Don't judge a book by its cover is a saying which probably ignored more than we ignore the terms & conditions of any app we sign up for. So, don't underestimate the power of an attractive, creative book cover.

Description: A good description sells a book like nothing else. They create anticipation, which convinces the reader to purchase it. A catchy title and an attractive cover can only get their attention – the description is what compels your audience into buying your book. It has to be absolutely perfect.

To paraphrase Winston S. Churchill, '**A good book description should be like a woman's skirt; long enough to cover the subject and short enough to create interest.**"

Reviews: Many authors share an exclusive pre-launch copy of their book with other writers, notable publications, and reviewers to get critical reviews. More than often, the reviews you receive will validate your book. You can even add snippets or blurbs to your cover to lure readers.

Number of Pages: There is always a defined range of page length bestselling authors follow. But you don't need to follow that necessarily. When it comes to earning millions of dollars, there are no set rules. You can either write 20 shorts books or just write one lengthy book. The downside of investing in one single book is increased liability. You are literally putting all your eggs in one basket. Twenty books on twenty different topics can target a wider range of topics, genres – bringing you closer to your goal of becoming a Passive income millionaire by earning money online.

Pricing: Now, this is a tricky part. You wouldn't want to undersell your book. Neither would you drive potential buyers away by putting up a really high price tag. The prices shouldn't be too high that only a small fraction of readers can afford it. Nor should It be too low to appear cheap and sub-standard.

To ensure your success, you need to ascertain the perfect price for your book. Study your target audience and their buying power. Another way to get your pricing right is to look at how much are other authors (in the same genre/sub-category) are charging for their eBooks.

Your book should be able to compel the reader to buy it in a go. It will help your book be on the list of bestsellers. If your story is interesting enough to capture the reader's attention, then these elements work as a cherry on top.

Decide Your Author Name

Once you have chosen a suitable genre and sub-category, the next step is deciding the author's name. Using your own name as the author seems to be the obvious choice. However, you do have the liberty to alter your name or choose an entirely new name for yourself.

You will need to specify your author name when publishing on Kindle Direct Publishing. Author name can either be your name or a 'Pen Name.'

The Concept of Pen Name

When writers or public personalities wish to remain anonymous, they opt for a pen name. Writers can keep their actual identity private if they don't want to be associated with their work.

A Pen Name is not a legal name and cannot be used for administrative purposes. It is a fictitious identity of a person. When using a Pen Name on Amazon, there are specific guidelines to follow. There are certain restrictions posed by amazon while using a pen name.

When to Use a Pen Name

Many writers use a pen name. It can either be because they don't want their name to be associated with their work or want to explore different genres with different identities. Some of the most common reasons why an author uses a pen name are:

- To protect their privacy while writing on politically or religiously sensitive topics.
- When they are writing on a genre that is different from their primary niche.
- If they are publishing for a company or website which demands the writer's anonymity.
- To protect their privacy or employment.
- To freely express their views without giving away their identity.
- To express their opinion on controversial subjects without getting a backlash from their peers.

In principle, a pen name is used to remain anonymous. Some authors use it to be creative and unique. A pen name also helps when an author is working on different genres and wishes to associate every genre with a distinct identity to increase credibility.

How to Create a Pen Name?

If you want to publish your work anonymously, then you can decide a pen name for yourself. Creating a pen name is easy and can be an exciting task for an author. You have the liberty to create a pen name from different sources, whether it is a combination of words you like or characters from your favorite novels or merely the name you would've given yourself if it was up to you. To create a pen name, you can pick the name of your favorite author or the name of your favorite character. Use a combination or make up a new name.

PART FOUR – Launching Your Product: Setting The Course for Success.

Overview

In this chapter, we will discuss how and where you can (and should) publish your book. Just like movies, pre-launch marketing plays an important role in the success of a book.

Create Pre-launch Buzz

If you want to earn millions of dollars online, you should not hold back at all. Give your book everything it needs to attract customers. Pre-launch marketing is a powerful way to boost your sales even before your book goes on sale. Create a buzz on the internet by using as many mediums you can. From social media to press releases, do everything you can to hype your book up before it hits the stores.

Social Media Ads

Facebook marketing is a cost-effective way to get pre-orders for your book. Create a landing page or posters for your book and promote it on Facebook. You can even target certain demographics on Facebook, which are more likely to be interested in ordering and reading your book.

Video Teasers

According to marketing experts, the engagement scores for video teasers is higher as opposed to text-based promotional material. Create a short 30-second teaser for your book. You can either make one yourself or hire someone from Guru.com or Fiverr.com to do it for you.

PART FIVE – Increase Your Passive Income: Identify patterns to Create Sales Funnels

Overview

The fifth and final chapter of the book highlights the significance of identifying sales patterns to increase your passive income. From researching market trends to developing new sales funnels, this chapter comprehensively addresses every aspect to empower you with the knowledge you *need* to earn millions. You are just **one step away** from becoming a millionaire through selling eBooks online.

What is a sales funnel?

Just like a funnel guides a liquid directly into a vessel, a sales funnel leads potential clients to your book – resulting in an exponential increase in sales. It involves a series of marketing actions (social media marketing, email marketing, landing pages, etc.), which essentially do all the work for you.

Now, to get it absolutely right, you need to develop the perfect sales funnel. Putting your book up for sale on Amazon can only get you an average flow of customers – but with the right sales funnel, you can accelerate and augment the volume of sales exponentially. From creating a website to deploying smart email marketing campaigns, there's a lot you can do to bring more money in.

Cost-effective Ways to Market Your Books

One of the easiest ways to increase your followers and create familiarity with your book, amongst other readers, is the strategies used for your book's promotions. Whether it is a press release, newsletter, or author swap, you need to try whatever fits in your promotion equation or try them all. Various websites help you with promotions according to the genre of your book. Here are a few simple ways to promote your book without spending a lot:

Email Marketing

Email marketing campaigns are probably the most old-school yet effective campaign to generate sales leads. But how does it work? Email marketing involves sending out mass emails to people who think this is it.

Social Media Marketing

With over 2 billion people on popular social media websites such as Facebook, Instagram, and Twitter, it does not make sense to not use social media to target a wider audience.

Landing Pages

Land more customers with an effective landing page. You can either hire the services of a freelance web designer/developer to make design an effective landing page for you. Or you could use a drag & drop service like Unbounce.

Press Release

Another way to increase your book's sales through promoting it is through writing a viral press release. You can hire a freelance writer from Fiverr and get it written in a few hours. This will not cost you much as well as help save you the hassle of writing the entire press release all by yourself.

Get multiple press releases written and distribute them to the most relevant digital and/or print outlets to get the word out. Generally, publications charge a nominal fee for sharing your press release – but it is worth every penny. Press releases not only play an important role in creating awareness about your latest book launches but also lend credibility to your profile as an author.

Newsletter Swaps

One of the organic ways to market your book to a wider audience is through newsletter swaps. When you enter this field of writing and publishing, it is essential that you socialize with other authors – regardless of their genre or standing in the literary circles. This will not only increase your network but also create new channels for the marketing of your book.

Furthermore, not only will it increase your exposure but also add new fans to your email list. It works both ways – quid pro quo – they promote your work, and you promote their work. Being a part of the author's network increases your credibility and gives your fans another reason not just to leave your emails unread. By giving them suggestions of new books by other authors, you will be able to grasp their attention, and they will most likely recommend your email subscription to other readers in their circle.

BONU$ SECTION – SHORT, EASY YET EFFECTIVE WAY TO EARN MONEY ONLINE

SHORT TIPS TO BECOME A MILLIONAIRE BY EARNING MONEY ONLINE

Focus on marketing – Many people think its smarter to do everything themselves – from writing the book to marketing it. While that may work for some, it isn't really the smart way to go about it. If you want to become a Passive income millionaire, you need to focus on creating as many sources of passive income as you can.

Target multiple niches – In the beginning, it is difficult to ascertain which genre is your forte. The best way to identify the best niche for you to work in is by targeting multiple niches at once! Rather than going with one lengthy eBook, opt for multiple short books. Once the sales stats come in, you will realize which niche is perfect for you.

Develop a robust outsourcing model – To earn a lot of money online, you need to let others do all the hard work for you. Develop a proper outsourcing model. Try to develop a team. Let's say you find a good writer on Fiverr or Guru.com for a really low price. Don't let them go after just one project and try someone new for every new project. This will not only save your time but also make the whole process a lot easier for you.

This page is intentionally left blank.

Passive Income Millionaire©
Almost everyone wants to earn millions but only a few know the secret to unlock a steady stream of passive income. But not anymore – passive income millionaire is set to transform the lives of its readers by revealing the ultra-secret, tried & tested method to earn real, honest money online.

If you are looking for a reliable and easy way to make money online, this book will tell you everything you need to know – and more!

www.ingramcontent.com/pod-product-compliance
Lightning Source LLC
Chambersburg PA
CBHW040327220526
45473CB00009B/2592